MW00907028

THIS BOOK BELONGS TO

____

____

59890141R00061

Made in the USA
Columbia, SC
09 June 2019